The Little Book of Garden Heroes

by Allan Shepherd

Additional research by Suzanne Galant
Additional material on plants, and technical edit, by Chloë Ward

D0754092

© CAT Publications 2004
The Centre for Alternative Technology Charity Ltd
Machynlleth, Powys, SY20 9AZ, UK
Tel. 01654 705980 Fax. 01654 702782
email: pubs@cat.org.uk web: www.cat.org.uk www.ecobooks.co.uk
Registered Charity No. 265239

The right of Allan Shepherd to be identified as the author of the work has been asserted
by him in accordance with the Copyright, Designs and Patents Act 1988. All rights
reserved. No part of this publication may be reproduced, stored in a retrieval system, or
transmitted, in any form or by any means, electronic, mechanical, photocopying, recording
or otherwise, without the prior permission of the copyright owner.

ISBN 1 90217 521 2
1 2 3 4 5 6 7 8 9 10

Design: Graham Preston
Illustrations: Katrina Moon

Mail Order copies from: Buy Green By Mail, Tel. 01654 705959
The details are provided in good faith and believed to be correct at the time of writing,
however no responsibility is taken for any errors. Our publications are updated regularly;
please let us know of any amendments or additions which you think may be useful for
future editions.

Printed in Great Britain by Welshpool Printing Group Ltd. (01938 552260)
on paper obtained from sustainable sources.

Cover photograpy: Seven spot ladybird *Coccinella 7-punctata* © Ken Preston-Mafham Premaphotos Wildlife

Dedication

Dedicated to my mum, Lesley, who looks after her own beautiful wildlife garden with the same care and love she gives to her children. And to Chloë, for inspiration and sharing her garden, and her love of garden heroes, with me.

Acknowledgements

I would like to thank first and foremost Suzanne Galant for her invaluable research and support, and Chloë Ward for advice and information. I would also like to thank my colleagues in the Publications Department at the Centre for Alternative Technology for allowing me the freedom to create this book. Lastly, I'd like to acknowledge the thousands of people who work, week in week out, to help protect and promote species threatened by extinction in Britain and throughout the world, and the gardeners, writers and scientists past and present who have contributed to our understanding of the natural world – without whom the writing of this book would not have been possible.

Contents

Introduction

Danger: Man @ work

From an early age I've been under the impression that ants (be they in the garden or not) are a bad thing and that a nest should be quickly disposed of with a jug of boiling hot water. As a young boy, and, if truth be told, an adult too, I have administered said painful death myself, but recently when I disturbed an ants' nest in my garden I decided to do nothing. I have vowed to let the ants live.

Since then, I've found seven nests and all of them are staying. This makes it difficult to lie on my lawn sometimes, so I've decided to buy a hammock. I've always wanted one anyway... People don't like ants in their garden because they are small, crawling things that interrupt picnics and occasionally give an irritating bite. Gardeners don't like ants because they protect aphid colonies from aphid predators and sometimes make their nests in inconvenient places, such as lawns. Even more occasionally they damage plant growth by undermining roots. However, they are also extremely good composters and this is reason enough to rein in that instinctive reach for the kettle. So long as leaves fall from the trees, there will always be ants in my garden.

I cannot say that I have developed any strong emotions regarding the ants in my garden, apart from curiosity, and even so I tend to leave well alone. I certainly wouldn't list them in my top ten all time favourite garden inhabitants. Although, faced with such a difficult task, I'm not sure what I would choose.

Seasoned garden naturalists may scoff at a list made too obvious by the inclusion of popular favourites such as the hedgehog, frog, butterfly and robin but I'm sure they would be there anyway. To please the elitists I might have to add something unusual, rather like the Desert Island Discs' guest who adds an aria from an obscure Icelandic composer in amongst the Mozart and Beethoven. Something like the spectacular thunder worm I found in the garden one day, and identified in a book: it looks like a self-propelling cotton thread.

Since I'm worried about those creatures endangered by human

activity, I would choose something listed in the Red Data Books of endangered species and, if it was in my power to do so, make some extra effort to help protect it. The Red Data Books now include a quarter of our native ladybirds, a quarter of Britain's 254 bee species, and hundreds of species of butterflies, birds, beetles and... Sadly, the list goes on and on. Choosing one from the list wouldn't be difficult.

I think I would pick a species of bee. I know I could quite easily encourage their survival in my garden. And as they are said to be responsible, through their unmanaged pollination services, for producing every third mouthful of human food, I really wouldn't want to see them disappear. I would choose the earthworm for its amazing qualities as a soil improver. Beyond that, the ladybird would get the nod...for its ability to munch aphids and its overall ability to enrich the gardening experience.

Coming from an organic gardening background, I've had it drummed into me not to think of gardening simply in terms of plants. Although plant growing is the ultimate goal of any gardener, an organic gardener knows that the plant must not be viewed in isolation but as part of a complete system. Hence the adage: feed the soil, not the plant.

This probably explains why I haven't yet mentioned a single plant. To my mind the plants almost go without saying. Gardeners need no encouragement to put plants in a garden, but they do need encouragement to make provision for the creatures that make the garden work properly. Especially as many of these garden creatures are threatened with extinction. The organic gardener needs to enlist the services of worms to improve soils (Chapter 1), insects to pollinate plants (Chapter 2), and predators to dispose of pests (Chapter 4). It doesn't take a leap of imagination to see that a garden wouldn't function properly if these species weren't around to do the valuable jobs they do. Thanks to European legislation, gardeners who previously resorted to chemical treatments also need to know more about the lives of these creatures. Many of the chemicals they used to use to do the job of defeating pests are no longer available (see page 120).

The organic gardener is also conscious that there should be room in the garden for plants that are beneficial to other plants and to the garden as a whole: plants that enrich the soil, and attract predators and pollinators. Since I've only got one place in my top ten left, my chosen plant has to be comfrey. Comfrey is rather an odd choice when there are so many beautiful flowers, fruits and vegetables to choose from, but you'll see why I've made this choice in Chapter 3.

The phrase 'garden heroes' seems to suggest that those plants and animals that benefit us are somehow consciously helping us out. Of course, this isn't true. They're just getting on with their own lives, and are far too busy in their 'universe' to worry about ours. It is a curiosity of nature that they happen to do the jobs we need doing and do them extremely well – and given the right conditions like to live in our gardens.

Man has a history of not appreciating, or even taking the time to find out about, such mutually beneficial relationships. We are nature's blunderers, not understanding our place in the natural order or taking much care of it. We enter unspoilt eco-systems with the force of a storm, and like the weather, give no thought to the consequences of our actions. There are thousands of historical examples to illustrate this point, but perhaps the two most famous are the stories of the dodo and the passenger pigeon, both now extinct.

In 1598 Admiral Cornelius van Neck and his crew of sailors disembarked on Mauritius, the island home of a strange flightless bird they christened 'dodoor' – the Dutch name for sluggard. Even though the dodoor was a 'Walkvogel', or disgusting bird, they set about eating it, because, being flightless, it was easy to catch. The Dutch used the island as a pasturing ground for livestock and even managed to offload monkeys and rats. Pigs destroyed the dodo's breeding grounds and the monkeys and rats consumed its eggs. As a result, after only 80 years of co-existence with humanity, the dodo became extinct.

In 1850, 5 billion passenger pigeons flew across the northern American states on their annual migration. Eyewitness accounts describe flocks a mile wide passing overhead without ceasing, for hours on end. Sometimes, when the birds flew over the crest of a hill they were simply clubbed out of the sky.

With the coming of the railway age the passenger pigeon became the easiest bird in America to catch and dispatch. Billions of dead birds were sent back to New York and the other great cities of the east coast, whose poor migrant workers relied on this cheap source of meat. In 1869 Van Buren County, Michigan, alone sent 7,500,000 birds east. By 1914, after consuming over 5 billion birds, America said goodbye to its last carrier pigeon. It died in captivity. One of the most impressive natural phenomena of the New World, gone for good.

Not that such tales are confined to the history books. Whilst writing this book the evidence that global warming, created by human activity, is causing or threatening to cause the extinction of many species has been arriving thick and fast. Those most immediately at risk are species that maintain a niche existence, dependent on stable climatic conditions, in very specific geographical areas. The golden toad of Costa Rica is one example, now thought to be the first creature to die out because of global warming. Closer to home, the seabirds on Orkney have raised no young this year because of food shortages. The fish they normally feed to their offspring have moved north, because the North Sea waters in which they previously lived are now too warm for them. Nature is giving us lots of signals that something is going terribly wrong.

And if the writing on the wall is already there for some species, the predictions for others are no less gloomy. The Royal Horticultural Society has already released a report suggesting that some of our finest plant collections will be endangered by a warmed climate. Some specialist gardens will have to consider moving their collections north if they are to survive. This climatic change is not a natural phenomenon...it is caused by us.

Most of us see the dodo as history's archetypal loser: the wrong bird in the wrong place at the wrong time. Few of us realise that the dodo was actually a victim of is own success. Having lived for thousands of years with no natural predator, it had no need for big, impractical and heavy wings. Instead it had evolved longer legs more suited to running across the forest floor on which it found its prey. Because of this it had what was to the human eye an ungainly look, which earned it unwarranted scorn. Lewis Carrolls' Will Guppy thought the dodo was 'invented for the sole purpose of becoming extinct, and that was all he was good for.' Our greatest hope is that some author of the future will still be here and won't be saying the same of 21st century Man.

This is not to say that it is too late for us to change our ways. We can all do something to help prevent climate change. We can make our homes more energy efficient, switch over to green electricity, travel less by car and aeroplane, and as gardeners choose organic and natural methods over chemicals. *The Little Book of Garden Heroes* is not about doing something about climate change (read CAT's *52 Weeks to Change Your World* for that). It is about providing the basic information you need to create a safe haven for the species we all rely upon to make our gardens both beautiful and effective. A little book like this cannot hope to contain all the information you will ever need on the subject. It is merely an introduction...a good starting point from which to develop a lifelong love for, and appreciation of, these special garden inhabitants.

Around the same time I first learned not to appreciate ants, the popular distraction of the time for boys of my age was 'Top Trumps'. These were sets of cards with names like, 'Tanks of the Great Powers', and the 'World's Biggest Cruise Ships'. My friends and I would sit around winning cards from each other by bettering the fire-power ratings of the tanks on the cards the others had in their hands. Looking back, I don't ever remember a pack called

'Great Garden Heroes'. In *The Little Book of Garden Heroes*, I have had my chance to put this right, whilst self-indulgently mimicking my own past – each of the four featured garden heroes now has its own 'top trump' card: the earthworm, the honey-bee, comfrey and the ladybird. It is meant primarily as a bit of fun (I am hereby issuing a disclaimer that the ratings given are not entirely scientific!), but it is also a way of remembering what an important part these creatures have played in both our history and culture, and of how much we would miss them if they disappeared. I hope you enjoy these diversions and indeed the rest of the book.

Part One
Garden Heroes

Chapter One

Composters: worms and other munchers

Sometimes humans have a wonderful way of adding value to something simply by their choice of names. A worm poo is called a casting or cast. The imagery this value added word conjures up – of worms producing tiny ingots of precious nutrients – is in this case entirely justified.

Worm casts contain high levels of those chemicals industry puts in fertilisers to help plants grow: potassium, nitrogen, and phosphorous. All these chemicals are found naturally in soil but some soils have less than others. If plants are grown in soils with low levels of any of these chemicals they are less likely to grow strong and resist disease. When present in the right balance (known as the NPK ratio, after their chemical symbols; i.e. Nitrogen (N), Potassium (P), Phosphorous (K)) they provide the gardening equivalent of three Shredded Wheat, or to use another breakfast analogy 'snap, crackle and pop'.

Top Trump – Earthworm

Scientific name:
Lumbricus terrestris

What we call it:
Earthworm

What the ancients called it:
Angel of the Earth

Historical significance:

History teachers love giving lessons about The Diet of Worms, 1521. In this case the Diet is a conference and Worms is a town in Germany: school children become very confused when they find out that a diet of worms resulted in the birth of the Protestant faith. Darwin doubted 'whether there are any other animals in the world which have played so important a part in the history of the world.'

Top Trump – Earthworm

Cultural high point:

Shakespeare couldn't get enough of them. Amongst Will's many worm related speeches, Romeo famously made worms' meat out of Mercutio, and Hamlet muttered rather madly, 'a man may fish with the worm that hath eat of a king, and eat of the fish that hath fed of that worm.' I like TW Connors' witty remark, 'She was one of the early birds and I was one of the worms,' and William Cowper's warning, 'I would not enter on my list of friends the man who needlessly sets foot upon a worm.'

Cultural low point:

'The Worm Has Turned': the Two Ronnies' mini-series where Englishmen escape a country run by women, by disappearing over the border to Wales, 'Where men are men and women are grateful.'

Top Trump - Earthworm

Weird fact you need to know: The worm starts to digest its food before it even enters its mouth. It does this by secreting a sticky fluid from the stomach onto the plant material. The liquid moistens and softens the leaves by destroying the starch in plant cells. The process of composting begins here and ends when the worm casts.

Key text from which this fact comes: *The Formation of Vegetable Mould Through the Action of Worms with Observations on Their Habits*, 1881, Charles Darwin. Darwin spent 39 years studying worms, amongst other things.

Top Trump - Earthworm

Value to gardener: 90% Although not essential to the composting process or gardening (ponds, hydroponics, pots and grow bags can all survive without them), no single creature is more useful to the organic gardener. As well as being a fabulous composter the worm creates a fine pattern of drainage channels in the soil and brings nutrients closer to the plants.

Ease of attraction: 80% Worms will avoid very dry soils and/or soils with no readily available food source.

Eye candy rating: 50% Not one of nature's beauty queens, but nevertheless a welcome sight.

Child friendly rating: 80% Children love worms. Some like eating them. Others will happily watch them in a home-made or bought wormery (see CAT Mail Order page 109).

Disclaimer: please note that this 'at a glance' rating system may not be entirely scientific!

Any new gardener will want to know something about their soil, primarily whether it is capable of sustaining their favourite plants. In some ways the gardener wishing to grow plants that encourage garden heroes has the advantage because these plants are overwhelmingly less fussy than other garden plants. A minority of garden plants truly prefer poor quality soil. However, this should not serve as an excuse for practising lazy soil care. Some of the trophy plants described later in this book thrive on good soil.

So what is 'good' soil...and if you haven't got it how do you get it? The two extremes of soil type are clay and sand, and most garden soils fall somewhere in between – with varying amounts of clay and sand making up the greater proportion of the volume of any soil. The perfect garden soil for the majority of plants is called loam. This has a good balance of clay and sand and the other main ingredient that makes up soil – organic matter. 90% of soil is rock (clay, sand, silt, slate and so on) and minerals. Some gardens are said to be stony because they have many visible pieces of stone in them (usually defined as particles of rock with a diameter greater than 2mm). The other 10% of soil is the organic fraction and whilst plants can absorb nutrients from the minerals and rock in garden soil they don't tend to do very well without organic material. This is the living part of soil. Rock, (with apologies to any Rolling Stones fans) is dead.

The life in this soil is extraordinarily rich. There are myriad life forms, in many 'universes' on scales ranging from the miniscule to the mammalian, constantly on the lookout for food, mates, air and water...from moles and worms right down to microscopic organisms, via insects such as ants and woodlice. The creatures of the soil are often described as a community and with good reason. In following their individual quests for life, they sustain each other. Plants form a symbiotic relationship with microscopic bacteria and fungi, which survive by attaching themselves to the roots of plants, then spend their time turning rotting matter into humus – a substance that provides the plants with the right sort of nutrients they need to survive.

The soil community and the invisible composters

Anyone who develops a passion for his or her soil should read Grace Gershuny's book *Start with the Soil* (see p.115). In it she suggests that every gardener should get to know how well their soil is doing by counting the number and types of creatures found within it. Worms, and other creatures visible to the naked eye, are a pretty obvious barometer of soil health, but if you want to know what's going on in the tiny 'universes' of invisible compost creatures you'll need to invest in a magnifying glass, or for serious studies a microscope. These microscopic creatures are 'king' decomposers and account for 60-80% of total soil life. As Grace Gershuny says, 'without them we would grind to a halt as we suffocated in our own wastes.' Some of them also have a very special relationship with plants, enabling the plant roots upon which they live to absorb nutrients from the soil. One example of this is the *Mycorrhizal* fungus that converts insoluble nutrients, most notably phosphorous, into biological forms usable by the host plant and receives, from the same plant, food in the form of carbohydrates.

The part the worm plays in this community is vital. Pockets of space filled with air (known as pores) account for 50% of the volume of good soil. Soil without pores is said to be compacted. Life in very compacted soils is hardly possible because most soil creatures need air. Compacted soils will not handle floodwaters well either. The channels and air pockets that allow air to permeate through the soil also allow water to flow freely. When a plant label says: 'Needs good drainage...' it is really saying you need a soil with air spaces and a thriving soil community.

Worms are great tunnellers. They spend their lives moving through soil, dragging decomposing material into it and through it, eating it and casting off poo. Darwin called them the 'intestines of the soil'. The tunnels they create allow air and water to flow freely through the soil. In hot weather worms retreat to deeper soils from which they will bring back nutrients for the rest of the soil community.

Worms are 80% water and although they can survive for days submerged in water they cannot survive a day isolated from it. Worms will leave very dry soils for more hospitable places.

Likewise, any soil without food will be an unattractive proposition. Although worms will live on freshly cut or rotting vegetation, meat, dropped leaves, the fallen petals of flowers and so on, Darwin found that the worms he used in his experiments had definite preferences. His worms preferred carrot tops to cabbage and liked sage, thyme and mint least of all.

Like all members of the soil community worms will only thrive in the right conditions. If your soil is of poor quality, either because it is compacted or because it has too much clay or sand or stone, the best way to improve it is to add material that will change its structure, provide the right sort of food, air and water levels for the soil community and put nutrients back into the soil for plants to access. The gardener can do this in several ways, for example by laying a mulch of organic material on top of the soil and allowing it to decompose into the soil, or by growing a green manure crop (see the section on beneficial plants). But the most effective method of all is to add compost.

Composting

Worms can live on nothing but moist kitchen scraps (excepting citrus fruits, which they don't like) and some people keep domestic wormeries to take full advantage of the speed at which a worm will compost them. However, before you set one up it's worth getting the low-down (see page 110). You'll need to get special worms, known as tiger or brandling worms, to do the job. (The temperature inside a wormery is much hotter than a normal compost heap and earthworms don't like it.) A brandling worm can eat around half its own body weight in kitchen scraps a day, and a wormery with a thousand worms can deliver a lot of worm casts. However, a wormery is a rather exclusive theatre of composting and a standard compost heap reflects more accurately the usual garden community. Enter stage left: ants, centipedes, flat top mites, fly larvae, fungi, millipedes, mites, astigmata mites, beetle mites, tortoise mites, nematodes, protozoa, pseudoscorpians, actinomycetes, algae, slugs, sow bugs, *Spirochetes* bacteria, springtails, *Staphylinidae* beetles, and woodlice ... composters all.

A wormery needs more regular attention than a conventional heap. Although it delivers compost much more quickly, the wormery keeper has to manage it, making sure the wormery is kept moist and keeping up with demands for food. Whether you choose a wormery or standard composting technique it helps to know that the composting creatures all need a healthy balance of carbohydrates, proteins, fats, vitamins and minerals, suitable living conditions and plenty of air and water to survive. It's your job to make sure they get what they want. And as they aren't all that fussy it's not too difficult. Composting creatures don't like squashed and waterlogged conditions and the best way to prevent this unwelcome development in your compost heap and/or wormery is to add cardboard and paper scraps.

The best way to collect cardboard and paper scraps is to get into a routine in the kitchen. Keep a dedicated container (a kitchen caddy) for collecting your cardboard and kitchen scraps (peelings, waste food etc.) and empty into your compost heap when full. If you don't like getting your hands dirty you can buy compostable bags made out of sweetcorn or potato starch, which can be tied at the top and lifted straight out of the kitchen caddy and put on the compost heap. Some people prefer not to compost meat, cooked food and bread but lots of people have no problem composting all of these.

Don't lay cardboard or paper flat in a compost heap. Instead scrunch up the cardboard into rough balls somewhere between the size of an egg and a small melon. Large pieces of cardboard, newspapers or magazines should be recycled rather than composted but smaller cardboard boxes (cereal packets, egg boxes etc.), paper towels, and the tubes from toilet rolls are all perfect.

One final hint about composting: separate garden waste according to size. Do not compost big twigs, branches and large plants and weeds in the same pile as grass cuttings, small weeds, and kitchen scraps and cardboard. If you haven't got room to compost bigger bits of waste take it off to a council green waste composting scheme.

A compost heap artificially encloses a naturally occurring phenomenon: the cycle of life and death. In the heap it is a process you have to manage. In the wild, composters aren't reliant on one single undertaker but a whole panoply of morticians. One of the best composting venues is the woodland. Here the seasons deliver to the forest floor fallen leaves, dying plants, rotting seeds, the shed skins of spiders, the abandoned pupae of caterpillars, the moulted hair of foxes, eggs fallen from the nest and an inexhaustible supply of poo of all shapes and sizes! Composting in a box is a fine pursuit but creating a garden that recreates some of the diversity of the cycle of life of the natural woodland is even better. Planting just one tree will enrich the life of the garden in so many ways: as well as bringing up nutrients from deeper soils it will provide cover for animals, a perch for birds, a home for insects, leaf mould for the soil, shade for humans and, of course, flowers for pollinating insects. Which brings us on to our next garden hero: the honey-bee.

Chapter Two

Pollinators: three bees and a butterfly garden

Honey-bees are cool: not only do they work co-operatively to one common aim, they mate in mid air and use the language of dance to tell each other where to go for a good meal. What do we have? Ronald McDonald... Moreover, they live in nature's answer to Darth Vader's Death Star, a spaceship so fiendishly designed it could only be destroyed by firing a missile down one very small service duct. And if this isn't enough to encourage us to celebrate the wonder that is the honey-bee it also produces...honey, and helps our flowering plants reproduce.

As a way of reproducing, pollination is both extraordinarily deliberate and random at the same time. Random because the whole thing relies on the dietary needs of an intermediary to ensure success and extraordinary because it actually works. It's worth reminding ourselves how the story goes: honey-bee needs food, is attracted by the sweet smelling, sugar-rich nectar in the flowers of plants, finds it deep within the flower, takes it, removes pollen (sperm) from the male organ of flower (stamen) as it does so, and hops on to the next flower for more food. Here it leaves pollen from flower a) on the female reproductive organ (stigma) of flower b), takes nectar, moves on. And that's it.

A little while later the plant develops seed and, depending on its predisposition, drops it where it stands, lets it fly on the breeze or gives it over to a carrier to dispose of some place else, quite often cushioned by a nice helping of 'poo' to encourage it to grow. Some pollinating plants are less sophisticated. They rely on the wind to distribute their pollen, releasing great clouds of the stuff up the noses of hay fever sufferers.

Top Trump – Honey-bee

Scientific name:
Apis mellifera

What we call it:
Honey-bee

What the ancients called it:
Small Messenger from God

Historical significance:

Bees! Which part of the historical record don't they crop up in? The ancient Greeks thought them priestly; Egyptians worshipped them as a symbol of the soul; Christians see them as a symbol of hope; Napoleon admired their organisational abilities; the Bourbons thought them kingly (at the time they didn't know the bee king was actually a queen!). It is also believed that our ancestors' migration from the forests of central Africa was only made possible by the exploitation of eco-systems already established as a result of the relationship between bee and flower.

Cultural high point:

Everybody likes honey. Everybody except Tiggers that is. Rupert Brooke wanted to know if there was still honey for tea, and the owl and the pussycat took onto their little pea green boat a big wad of cash and some honey. Man inhabits a Biblical land of milk and honey and Jonathan Swift noted that we had 'chosen to fill our hives with honey and wax: thus furnishing mankind with the two noblest of things, which are sweetness and light.'

Cultural low point:

The Bee Gees; Julie Andrews' 'When the bee stings, when I'm feeling bad'; the beehive hairdo (unless its worn by Marge Simpson); Sting.

Top Trump – Honey-bee

Weird fact you need to know: Bees will fly over a field full of inferior agricultural rape nectar to reach a garden full of the good stuff, so plant the flowers bees love: lavender, rosemary, thyme, nasturtium, poached-egg flower,  snapdragon, sunflower, Virginian stock, chives, fennel and oriental poppy are just some of the options you have.

Value to the gardener: 50% Honey-bees are great pollinators but they lose percentage points for being just one species in a crowd. There are many sub-species of bee, such as the Red Mason and bumble-bee (see below) and there are hover-flies, flies, wasps, ladybirds and butterflies. Also, if your garden consisted entirely of ferns and mushrooms you would have no need for pollinators at all. Having said this, according to bee expert Christopher O'Toole, (see page 116) every third mouthful of human food depends on the unmanaged services of bees.

Top Trump – Honey-bee

Ease of attraction: 70% Your efforts may be hampered by your location. However many bee friendly plants you have, if you haven't got a colony near your house you may be starved for honey-bee company. Still you won't know until you try...

Eye candy rating: 70% Only those who suffer an intense allergic reaction to bee stings and children and adults who try to swat them can fail to get pleasure from seeing bees in the garden.

Child friendly rating: 50% Some children love them and some just don't. They find bees fascinating to watch so long as they don't dive bomb their fizzy pop or precipitate the dropping of ice-cream on to the floor or their clothes as a previously interested child desperately flicks the bee away from the treat they've been looking forward to all day. (Guess whose day out to the seaside was spoiled by that particular incident... Still, that was probably a wasp.) The Red Mason bee (see page 46) is a good 'pet' to encourage in the garden because it will only sting under severe duress, and is not as aggressive as the honey-bee.

And so on to the Death Star, the bees' home: the hive. The first thing to know about beehives is that each one has its own distinctive hive smell. If a bee from another hive or any other insect gets through the single tiny entrance to the hive, which is always patrolled by guard bees, their presence will soon be detected because they just won't smell right. Singling them out for extermination, the resident bees will synchronise a massive counter-attack on the intruder by releasing alarm pheromones.

Bees are very clean animals and will remove any unwanted debris, such as the limp body of a dead intruder, very quickly. So-called undertaker bees, whose primary function is to remove the hundred or so corpses of those comrades who fall down dead on the job every day, will be called upon to carry the intruder out. Once outside they are unceremoniously dumped and left for the worms.

Each honey-bee has a specific and non-negotiable role to play in the hive. As this is determined before birth there's no room for the nature-v-nurture debate here. Bees are born to be queen, worker or drone. No guesses as to which sounds the most attractive option, but it's pretty lonely at the top and the queen bee has to survive insecticide at birth or in early childhood (killed by a rival), banishment, or a constant struggle to maintain her position. On the plus side, a queen bee gets a better diet and has a life expectancy of three years (compared to a month for workers). The queen has the added responsibility of maintaining the balance of the hive – determining the sex and therefore the occupation of her offspring before they are born.

Female bees generally become workers. In the short month of the worker bee's life, there are 12 days of cleaning, nursemaiding and serving as a lady-in-waiting to the queen, 8 days of packing nectar and building honeycomb, and ten days (the last ten) foraging for nectar. Males have but one purpose: to mate with the queen. After they do, they die, their genitalia detached and left inside the queen. 85 of 100 bees will be workers (which includes the undertakers), 14 will be mates and one will be queen.

Having spent the first 20 days of their life in the hive, it's not surprising that worker bees make the most of their sojourn in the great outdoors. Flying at up to 15 miles per hour, they can travel three-and-a-half miles in a single flight, visiting thousands of flowers on the way. If bees had egos the high point of their lives would be the discovery of a new supply of nectar. This provides them with the opportunity to dance 'the waggle' in front of the rest of the hive, on a special dance floor set aside for the purpose.

The waggle consists of a figure of eight movement with a straight 'walk' in between the loops and a sporadic fluttering of wings. A bee can perform the waggle just once, a hundred times, or anything in between, in one dance. The bees crowded round to watch the dance will leave as soon as possible to find the nectar, the site of which is indicated by the waggle. If a bee waggles only a few times the nectar source is close to the hive. The more waggles the bee performs the further the other bees will have to travel to exploit the new source of food. Scientists have determined that every 75 milliseconds' worth of waggle adds roughly another 330 feet in distance travelled.

Spectator bees will also study carefully the angle of the dancer's waggle walk – the bit in between the figure of eight loops. The dancing bee creates an imaginary line from the dance floor to the sun and shows the direction of the food source by deviating from it using precise measurements of angles. If the food is 10% to the left of the line the bee walks 10% to the left of the line. If it lies in the exact direction of the sun, the bee will walk straight up. At the close of the dance the dancer shares the smell of the flowers' pollen with the crowd, who sample it one by one with their antennae.

A bee will not wait to watch more than one other bee dance. The worker bee knows that procrastination is not good for the hive. There's no waiting for something better to come along. A bee makes hay while the sun shines, because during the winter months a hive will dine on two pounds of honey a week. As worker bees live no longer than four weeks this dedication to the survival of the hive is an incredible testimony to communal altruism, especially when you consider that an average worker bee will make no more than one twelfth of a teaspoon of honey in its whole life. Truly heroic behaviour...

The bee's sense of urgency seems to drive the rest of the garden. Plants that rely on these intermediary pollinators seem to sense the nature of this battle for resources and, trying to find a unique selling point, will compete with their neighbours to produce brighter flowers, and nectar that is sweeter and more plentiful than that of their rivals.

Some flowers have even responded to the needs of particular bees by evolving to suit those bees. The foxglove, for example, has arranged things so that the bumble-bee starts at the bottom of its tower of flowers (where the female flowers lie) and works its way up. By the time it reaches the male flowers at the top of the tower the bee is getting less and less nectar, as carefully arranged by the foxglove, and decides to move on to the bottom of the tower of the next plant, thus bringing the male pollen of one plant to the female flowers of another.

Red Mason Bee

Only the very dedicated Pooh Bears amongst you will want to manage your own man-made honey-bee hive. For those of you who like the idea of keeping your own 'pet' bees, but don't want to don the protective garb of the bee wrangler and actively generate honey, the Red Mason bee could be the answer. Unlike the honey-bee the Red Mason is a solitary creature, living alone in her nest and never getting to see her offspring. Actually there are far more solitary bees like the Red Mason than sociable ones. The Red Mason bee belongs to a family of bees that are known as cavity nesters. By nature they choose hollow plant stems and beetle boreholes in dead wood.

Mostly they prefer mature hedgerows but, with their gradual disappearance, the garden is becoming an increasingly important reserve. Christopher O'Toole, who has spent thirty years studying wild bees, has found them nesting in discarded garden canes, disused locks in greenhouses, holes in large pieces of flint, nail holes in old fence posts and spaces amongst thatch and roofing tiles. He has designed (with the Oxford Bee Company) a Mason bee nest you can buy for your garden. A sheltered east facing spot that gets the early morning sun is the ideal place for a nest but, as long as you don't face it north, any protected place will do. The life of the Red Mason bee, as described by Christopher O'Toole in his book on the subject, is just as fascinating as that of the honey-bee.

The Bumble-bee

It may not produce the sort of honey we prefer, but the bumble-bee is no sluggard when it comes to helping us get what we want. The bumble-bee can do something the honey-bee cannot. It can buzz pollinate. Tomatoes, peppers and aubergines store their pollen in a chamber within their flower and it can only be released by the high frequency wing muscle vibration of a bumble-bee. The bee has to cling on to the flower, position itself to get a covering of pollen when it is finally released, and vibrate like there's no tomorrow. This ability to buzz at the required rate is not a feather in the honey-bee's cap, which is why commercial growers choose to site bumble-bee and not honey-bee colonies close to their glasshouses and polytunnels. The bumble-bee is long tongued, which means that it can access flowers denied its shorter tongued cousins. Bumble-bees were exported to New Zealand in the 1890s to help pollinate clover grown for cattle and sheep. Despite their economic value, 5 species of bumble-bee are now on the Red Data Book list of endangered species thanks to intensive agricultural practice and the loss of hedgerows. Gardeners can do their bit to improve this situation by planting bumble-bee friendly species. Christopher O'Toole provides the following list: comfrey (see next chapter), yellow archangel, white deadnettle, red deadnettle, sage, thyme, marjoram, rosemary, lavender, lamb's ear, skullcap, bugle, geranium, snapdragon, toadflax, sweet pea, buddleia, foxglove and purple toadflax. It is important to grow a variety of plants so that flowers are provided throughout the season. English nature's leaflet 'Help Save the Bumble-bee' includes a list of plants for all seasons and some good advice on providing the right sort of habitat. As for the Red Mason bee, you can buy a bumble-bee home from the Oxford Bee Company via CAT (see page 109).

The Butterfly Effect

Butterflies have an ethereal quality lent by their fragility. Some mythologians have likened them to fairies; to the Greeks they represented the departing soul of the dead. In paying homage to a fellow poet, Frederico Garcia Lorca wrote, 'Not for a moment, beautiful aged Walt Whitman, have I failed to see your beard full of butterflies.' Butterflies are fussy creatures. As caterpillars they depend on particular food plants – as butterflies, favoured flowers for nectar, the two usually quite different. The comma caterpillar eats nettle, hop and elm leaves. The small tortoiseshell, red admiral and peacock caterpillars only eat nettle and the painted lady caterpillar likes nothing but thistles. You can only hope that your neighbour's garden has plenty of these so you can concentrate on growing hebe for the adult painted lady. If you don't want anything to do with thistles and nettles, small whites love the easy to grow and attractive nasturtium both as caterpillar and butterfly. Several butterflies like herbs such as marjoram, lavender, thyme and sweet rocket and the buddleia is commonly called the butterfly bush. A garden grown for butterflies can be very beautiful and watching them flit about throughout the summer months is a real treat. If you want to know how to grow one contact Butterfly Conservation for more information (see p 112). Be careful though, prolonged mixing with these delicate creatures could bring about some strange results. You don't want to end up like Chuang Tsu, who wrote the following, at least two centuries before the birth of Christ: 'I do not know whether I was then a man dreaming I was a butterfly or whether I am now a butterfly dreaming I am a man.' Or perhaps you do...

Flowers also work hard to meet the often quite particular tastes of other pollinators, including hover-flies, flies, wasps, ladybirds and butterflies. The Comma butterfly prefers nectar from the flower of the devil's-bit scabious, a name that sounds like it ought to belong to the sort of band John Peel introduces on his late night Radio One show.

Chapter Three

Plants: heroic herbs and the 'compost plant'

Whilst it may not be the most distinguished, aromatic or colourful plant in the garden, no single herb is more valuable to the gardener than Russian comfrey. Its use is certainly not as a gastronomic plant. Its rough and hairy adult leaves are best left for cows, pigs and giraffes (it is good for their bones). Although younger leaves can be sneaked into a spring salad, cooked as a vegetable in a soup, creamed with eggs to make a soufflé, liquidised to a juice, ground to a flour and infused for tea, the Royal Horticultural Society advise against it because of fears about toxicity. Unlike other common garden herbs it is not generally used to enhance the taste of a meal either. It is not common practice to nip out from the kitchen for a sprig of comfrey. For last minute flavouring we rely on other herbs such as rosemary, thyme, oregano and basil.

Nor is the average gardener likely to benefit much from its therapeutic value, even though this is considerable. Herbalists throughout history have used comfrey as a poultice to set bones and heal wounds. It is still used by modern herbalists but chemists tend to use a synthesised version of allantoin – the chemical, found naturally in both common and cultivated comfrey, responsible for the healing process. Whilst it is possible to make comfrey flour poultices, tea and ointments it is probably safer to contact a registered herbalist (contact HDRA for details, see page 112) if you are considering harnessing its medical properties.

The reason Russian comfrey is such a good plant to have around is that it is the closest thing we gardeners have to a compost producing plant. It is remarkable in that it has almost the same chemical composition as compost (ten parts carbon to every one part nitrogen). Moreover it has very high levels of NPK, just like our old friend the worm cast. In fact, according to analysis of its NPK content (either wilted comfrey leaf or finished comfrey compost) it outperforms farmyard manure and ordinary compost. It is also one of the easiest plants in the world to propagate and can deliver four or five harvests a year. And as if this wasn't enough, its nectar is harvested by bumble-bees.

Top Trump – Comfrey

Scientific name:
Symphytum x uplandicum

What we call it:
Russian comfrey

What the ancients called it:
The wild common comfrey
variously nicknamed knitbone,
boneset, bruisewort
and nipbone.

Historical significance:
Although common comfrey had
been popular with herbalists
for over two thousand years
not much is known of the
history of cultivated Russian
comfrey before 1771. This is
the year Hackney nurseryman
Joseph Busch landed the job of
Catherine the Great's head
gardener at the Palace of St
Petersburg. Within a few years
plants grown from the cuttings
he sent back home could be
found all over Britain.

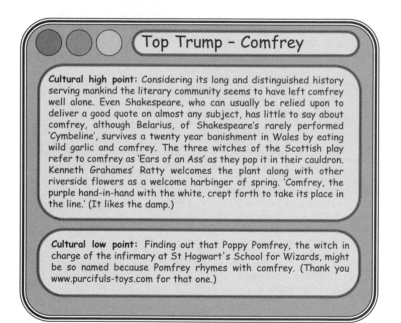

Top Trump – Comfrey

Cultural high point: Considering its long and distinguished history serving mankind the literary community seems to have left comfrey well alone. Even Shakespeare, who can usually be relied upon to deliver a good quote on almost any subject, has little to say about comfrey, although Belarius, of Shakespeare's rarely performed 'Cymbeline', survives a twenty year banishment in Wales by eating wild garlic and comfrey. The three witches of the Scottish play refer to comfrey as 'Ears of an Ass' as they pop it in their cauldron. Kenneth Grahames' Ratty welcomes the plant along with other riverside flowers as a welcome harbinger of spring. 'Comfrey, the purple hand-in-hand with the white, crept forth to take its place in the line.' (It likes the damp.)

Cultural low point: Finding out that Poppy Pomfrey, the witch in charge of the infirmary at St Hogwart's School for Wizards, might be so named because Pomfrey rhymes with comfrey. (Thank you www.purcifuls-toys.com for that one.)

Top Trump – Comfrey

Weird fact you need to know: If you place a layer of comfrey leaves just beneath the soil under potato plants the finished crop will taste better – that's according to comfrey expert Lawrence D. Hills who bred the most popular form of domestic comfrey, Bocking 14. In 1960 he ran a blind taste test and found that 16 out of 28 people preferred the taste of the 'comfried' potatoes. Other potatoes in the test were grown with ordinary compost, farmyard manure and chemicals. The only person who thought that the potatoes grown using chemicals tasted better was a smoker.

Key text from which this fact was gleaned: *Comfrey: Past, present and future* by Lawrence D. Hills. Second hand copies available via www.amazon.co.uk

Value to the gardener: 70% You don't need comfrey to garden organically but it makes life a lot easier having it around. Any gardener looking for a soil improver will find growing comfrey is quicker than compost making and cheaper than buying a chemical alternative.

Ease of growing: 80% It's difficult to go wrong with comfrey. You can order a root cutting through the post from www.organiccatalog.com (0845 130 1304) or take a cutting from a friend's plant (see below). Lawrence D. Hills preferred to grow it in full sun away from trees and hedges but if you're not worried about maximising quantity, it will grow quite happily in most places, including orchards. It loses quite a few per cent because it will not grow in peat or in thin soils, where rock lies a foot or so beneath the surface. Its deep roots need a good three to four feet of soil to play with.

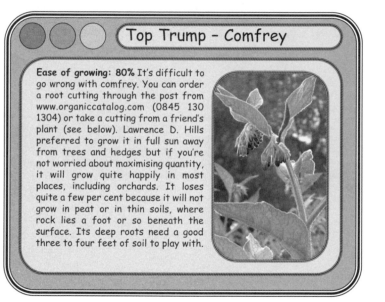

Top Trump – Comfrey

Eye candy rating: 60% Not the most attractive of plants, but by no means ugly. As Ratty noted, it has welcoming flowers. Although it will fit quite happily into any herbaceous border, as one of the taller, beefier cultivated plants it is often put at the edges of a garden to act as a barrier bouncer against creeping weed invasions. Its big leaves can provide shelter for more delicate plants. Putting it next to a compost heap is a good option. Not only will its pretty flowers and attractive green leaves act as camouflage for the bin, but also it will soak up the nutrients that leak from the compost.

Child friendly rating: 30% In a garden full of interesting plants it will probably look a little dull. Its hairy leaves can cause irritation to the skin too so, although it's nowhere near as troublesome as the nettle bed you need to plant for your butterflies, it's probably best to put it where children aren't going to get too close. Alternatively, just tell them it will irritate them if they play around with it.

The key to comfrey's success is the size of the plant's roots, which push down deeper into the soil than many other plants. The comfrey plant uses its roots to take up minerals, nutrients and water sources from deep soils other plants can only dream about. It may be the gardening equivalent of a Hungarian weight lifter but its brutishness masks sophisticated survival techniques.

Once absorbed through the comfrey's roots, nutrients and minerals are transferred to the leaves, which can then be cut and, through the various methods described below, made available to other plants in the garden. This redistribution of soil wealth is known as dynamic accumulation. In theory, all plants are dynamic accumulators but some are much better at it than others. Most plants in growth rob more nutrients and minerals from the soil than they can give back, and we have to add compost to garden soil to make up for their imprudence and our desire to grow 'greedy' plants.

The organic vegetable gardener has to take care of his/her soil by making sure crops are rotated so that good dynamic accumulators follow the not so good ones. Greedy crops such as cabbage and broccoli may be followed one year by nitrogen fixing broad beans the next. If the gardener wants to give the soil an added boost green manure crops such as alfalfa, mustard and clover will be grown, cut and dug back in. Most dynamic accumulators, such as borage and marigold, only accumulate one or two minerals. Comfrey is one of the most efficient, bringing up from deep soils silica, nitrogen, magnesium, calcium, potassium and iron, all of which are good for plant vitality. But even comfrey is not as good as the dandelion, which brings up sodium and copper as well. Interestingly there are several weeds that dynamically accumulate for the benefit of the rest of the garden: chickweed and dock being the best.

Cultivating Comfrey

Comfrey is one of the easiest plants in the world to grow. You can grow it from seed but it is easier to grow from a piece of root cut from a plant. You won't need much: about four inches of root 0.5 inches thick is plenty. If you get your root cutting from any source other than a commercial supplier make sure it's not wild comfrey, as this will spread like a weed, coming up in lots of places you don't want it. Commercially grown comfrey can be controlled because it is sterile. Bocking 14 is the connoisseur's choice, delivering the best figures for mineral uptake.

Plant your root cutting in March, April or May – or if you miss the spring, in September. The earlier you plant the greater the harvest that year. Root cuttings should be placed just beneath the soil. Young plants can be eaten by slugs so you may wish to start off your comfrey in a pot and plant it out when the leaves are at least six – twelve inches high. Whether you are planting your root cutting in a pot or straight into the soil try and plant it so that any new shoots are pointing upwards. If you can't see any shoots and don't know which end is going to produce them lay the root horizontally. Leave gaps of two feet between each plant. When your root starts to send shoots up through the surface of the soil, hoe around and between plants (if you've more than one). Within six weeks you can cut the first growth down to an inch or so above the ground. As the year goes on just repeat the cut every six weeks.

What you do with your cut leaves is a matter of choice. Leaves from the first cut (left to wilt for a day or two) can be placed slightly under the soil at the bottom of a potato trench. Tests show that comfrey used in this way will increase yields. If your first leaves are ready a little later in the season they can be placed around the potato plants. If you are not growing potatoes and don't want to process the comfrey in any way, you can just lay the leaves on the ground around any plants. Eventually they will be eaten by composters and disappear into the soil. While the leaves keep their shape they will suppress some of the less determined weeds, keep moisture in the soil and attract slugs (which you can remove and dispose of).

The next easiest option is just throwing it onto the compost heap. Comfrey is a really good compost activator, as it is much enjoyed by compost creatures. If you grow a lot of plants in pots you can create your own comfrey potting compost by mixing alternate 3-4 inch layers of leaf mould and chopped comfrey leaves in a black plastic sack. Leave it in there for 2-5 months but check that the mixture does not dry out or become waterlogged. After that time it should be ready to use as a general potting compost, but it can be too strong for seedlings.

Don't compost comfrey on its own though, it just turns into sludge. If you're going to turn comfrey into sludge you should do it in a bucket and use the resultant liquid as a fertiliser. This does however require a small amount of engineering skill, a knowledge of rudimentary 'bucketometry' and a determined nose. The bucket contents tend to stink after a while, so keep it away from the house and out of the reach of children. Keep it covered too. Without a lid it can become a breeding ground for insects. Writing this, the whole process doesn't sound too attractive, but the liquid fertiliser is a worthy prize.

It takes four or five weeks to produce a comfrey concentrate ready for use. You'll need to make a stand arrangement that allows the comfrey liquid to drop through a small hole in the bottom of the comfrey bucket and into another bucket underneath.

This allows you to use the concentrate without disturbing the first bucket, which you can then refill time after time. Having a large heavy object pressing down on the comfrey within the first bucket facilitates the speedier descent of liquid into the second bucket. The drawback is you'll have to remove said large heavy object each time you want to fill it up with more comfrey. The comfrey concentrate in the second bucket can then be added to a watering can. HDRA, the organic organisation, recommend one part comfrey concentrate to every 15 parts water. Use it on tomatoes or peppers three times a week, other greenhouse plants twice a week, and pot plants and outdoor hanging baskets once a week.

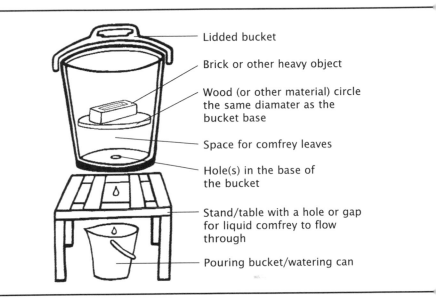

Lidded bucket

Brick or other heavy object

Wood (or other material) circle the same diamater as the bucket base

Space for comfrey leaves

Hole(s) in the base of the bucket

Stand/table with a hole or gap for liquid comfrey to flow through

Pouring bucket/watering can

One option for those of a delicate disposition is to place their cut comfrey leaves at the bottom of a lidded water butt with a tap, and siphon off the resultant comfrey tea. If you've got a full butt you shouldn't have to dilute the liquid (about 7kg of comfrey to 100 litres of water is about the right proportion). If you find the comfrey blocks the flow of water through the tap you may need to engage the use of a large stick to whoosh the comfrey up a bit or perhaps put a filter (old tights or net curtain) over the tap inlet. Both comfrey concentrate and comfrey tea will provide a welcome nutrient and mineral hit for any plant.

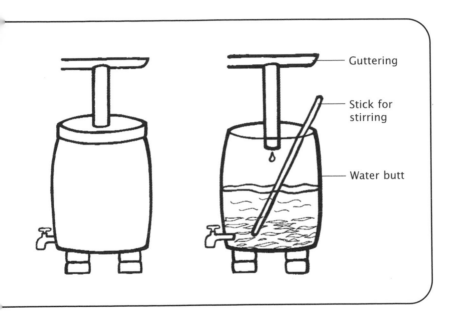

Guttering

Stick for stirring

Water butt

It is not possible to list here the hundreds of plants suitable for encouraging wildlife (for such a list you should pick up the English Nature leaflet 'Plants for Wildlife Friendly Gardens'). Instead I asked wildlife gardener Chloë Ward to pick out a handful of those plants she considers most beneficial to the average garden. I asked her to limit her choice of plants to those that most people could grow in most gardens in most soils with great ease. The following few pages are hers.

Poached egg plant – *Limnanthes douglassii*

The poached egg plant looks, when in flower, as its name suggests, like masses of tiny poached eggs covering the ground at a height of about six inches. It is a charming looking hardy annual and very easy to grow from seed. Once established, it will self seed happily and stay around year after year. Ground covering plants are friends in our gardens because they smother young weed seedlings, and prevent soil erosion and water loss.

It's not just pretty ground cover, though, but also a superb hover-fly attractant; and hover-flies are superb aphid controllers. Bees love the flowers too and while visiting will pollinate your fruit and veg. This makes *Limnanthes* especially useful when grown under and between fruit trees and bushes and in among vegetables. So cover your ground in *Limnanthes* and the poached egg plant will see to it that your weeds are controlled, your fruit pollinated and your aphids eaten!

Stinging nettle – *Urtica dioica*

Not all of us welcome the nettle into our gardens – but we should. For if we want to see butterflies gracing our flower borders we need to provide not only nectar but also egg laying sites. Insects are very particular in where they want their young to begin life and for the red admiral, small tortoiseshell and peacock butterflies, only the nettle will do. Nettles are also home to early aphids. By encouraging a population of aphids early in the spring, we entice in their predators, e.g. hover-flies and ladybirds, who will then move on to eat the aphids on our broad beans and soft fruit later in the year.

The nettle, though, isn't just food for insects. Many people like to eat it too. It is rich in iron and young leaves make a very nice nettle soup (check for caterpillars first, though). Other plants also appreciate the goodness of nettles. That is, the stems and leaves can be used in a similar way to comfrey, i.e. added to your compost heap, made into a liquid feed or used as mulch. They are less rich in potassium than comfrey, but richer in nitrogen. Therefore, use nettles on plants where strong leaf growth is needed.

So, make space for nettles! Grow them in a pot if you are worried about them spreading. Or, if you keep a patch, cut them back occasionally as you harvest for your soup/tea/mulch/compost. Cut different sections back at different times to encourage fresh growth throughout the summer. Your butterflies will appreciate it.

Crimson-flowered broad bean – *Vicia faba*

Believe it or not, some vegetables are being persecuted by the establishment. To sell any seed that is not on a special EU approved seed list has been declared illegal. This means that many old and interesting vegetable varieties are no longer in the shops and are therefore in danger of dying out. The crimson-flowered broad bean very nearly became extinct, but was rescued and brought back into cultivation by the Heritage Seed Library (HSL) run by the Henry Doubleday Research Association (HDRA see page 112). The HSL overcome these crazy laws by giving away seed to members who then grow the plants and return some of the saved seed to the library, thus ensuring the survival of those varieties.

So, the crimson-flowered broad bean deserves a place in our hearts and gardens just for being a survivor, but it also looks stunning when in flower and provides us with numerous small upright pods of tender beans.

Need another reason to love it? OK, it makes our soil more fertile. As a member of the pea and bean family, the broad bean has nodules on its roots where nitrogen-fixing bacteria live. These bacteria take nitrogen from the air and convert it into a form that plants can use. So, after the beans have been harvested (and seeds saved) the next plants to take up residence in their place will benefit from extra nitrogen in the soil. Thus the earth becomes a little richer when the broad bean is grown.

Honeysuckle – *Lonicera periclymenum*

It's not called honeysuckle for nothing; the flowers really do give forth sweet nectar when sucked from the base. Honeysuckle is a serious source of food for garden wildlife. The flowers, being night-scented, are designed to attract moths as pollinators. Not many of us get to know night-flying insects (because we are in bed/in front of the telly/out clubbing when they are out and about) but they perform the same vital functions as more familiar daytime insects. The moths are in turn food for bats, harmless but persecuted mammals, which need all the help they can get (since most of the 14 British species are now classified as endangered).

The entwined mass of the plant gives good cover for birds and small mammals. If you are lucky enough to live in an area still inhabited by dormice, the honeysuckle will provide them with much needed food (flowers and fruit). The berries are food for many bird species including warblers, thrushes and bullfinches.

There are all sorts of fancy varieties of honeysuckle sold in garden centres, but our simple native will look beautiful grown against a wall or scrambling up a tree, and is still available in its pure form from wildflower nurseries (including Naturescape: 01949 860592, www.naturescape.co.uk).

Elder – *Sambucus nigra*

Every garden needs a tree. All plants have their uses, but trees do more to absorb greenhouse gases, give habitat to wildlife, and shade us from UV light than other plants – because in this case, size does make a difference. It's a very hard task to single out one tree, and many would go for the grand old oak or majestic beech, but let's hear it for the humble elder...

Small enough to fit in any garden (although they can grow to 10m if unrestricted by space or human intervention) – even if your garden is a bucket – the elder is easily grown and will reward you greatly with a bounty of goodies. In spring the edible flowers can be enjoyed raw or battered, to make flower-fritters or 'frizzets', or used to make elderflower 'champagne' or cordial. But don't pick them all, some need to be left to form berries for wine-making. Wildlife enjoys all these treats, too, so share your flowers with the insects and your berries with the birds.

The elder is the tree of the fairies and is said to repel flies, and, if necessary, the devil. So be good to your elder and it will be good to you.

Chapter Four
Predators: ladybirds and other crunchers

The Ladybird

Gosh life is difficult sometimes. How do you pick an archetypal garden predator when there are so many to choose from, and so many of them doing different but nevertheless vital jobs? Well, quite frankly, it's easier to illustrate an argument about natural born killers by picking one that's known and loved by everybody. However, even in this category, there are quite a few contenders. Hedgehog, frog and any number of favourite garden birds such as robin, wren or blackbird could vie for the job. What is it about cuddly killers? In the end I've plumped for the ladybird because of its awesome appetite for aphids.

Like slugs, aphids are both troublesome and fascinating. They are such a strange mix of the miraculous and the mundane. On the one hand they spend all their time sucking the sap from plants. On the other they are parthenogenetic. Most of us are taught about the birds and the bees at school, but who ever had a lesson in the miraculous multiple virgin birth of the aphid? Forget human cloning, it's already happening, right here in aphid world. The aphid female gives birth to nymphs that are her clones without any need for males. Even more awesome is the fact that these little nymph clones come into the world complete with their own clone babies partially developed inside them.

Not only is this a smart way of ensuring one's genes get passed on to two generations in one go, it enables whole populations of aphids to replicate much more quickly than the predators who eat them (who normally breed conventionally and at a much slower rate). A ladybird for example breeds annually. Colonies of aphids can increase ten- to twenty-fold in a week at the height of summer.

Organic gardeners don't spray their aphids with chemicals because the chemicals kill off the predators, who are unable to recover at the same speed as the pest. A few generations of sap suckers will make short shrift of a plant. Not only will the removal of sap harm the plant's overall well-being, the stuff that comes out of the other end of the aphid blocks up the plant's pores and leads to the growth of moulds. This substance has the value added title honeydew and is a tasty treat for ants (who, wisely, farm the aphids by protecting them from predators such as ladybirds).

Top Trump – Ladybird

Scientific name:
Coccinellidae

What we call it:
Ladybird

Historical significance:

Ladybirds may not have changed world history but they've certainly taken their place in folklore. If you don't get good luck when one lands on your hand you must have been born cursed... The deeper the red and the more spots on the back of that ladybird the greater the fortune.

What the ancients called it: Christians might have named it after the Virgin Mary (Our Lady), but it didn't stop some in Italy calling it the Devil's Chicken. For what reason I know not. Lancastrians call them God's Horses; Yorkshire folk, Dowdy Cows; the Welsh, Red Cows of God; and the Spaniards, God Almighty's Cow.

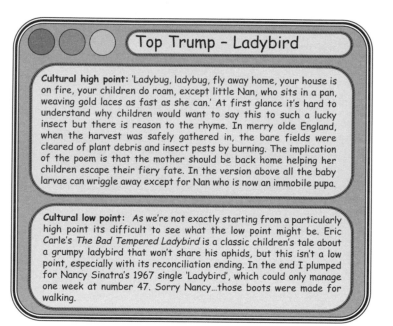

Top Trump – Ladybird

Cultural high point: 'Ladybug, ladybug, fly away home, your house is on fire, your children do roam, except little Nan, who sits in a pan, weaving gold laces as fast as she can.' At first glance it's hard to understand why children would want to say this to such a lucky insect but there is reason to the rhyme. In merry olde England, when the harvest was safely gathered in, the bare fields were cleared of plant debris and insect pests by burning. The implication of the poem is that the mother should be back home helping her children escape their fiery fate. In the version above all the baby larvae can wriggle away except for Nan who is now an immobile pupa.

Cultural low point: As we're not exactly starting from a particularly high point its difficult to see what the low point might be. Eric Carle's *The Bad Tempered Ladybird* is a classic children's tale about a grumpy ladybird that won't share his aphids, but this isn't a low point, especially with its reconciliation ending. In the end I plumped for Nancy Sinatra's 1967 single 'Ladybird', which could only manage one week at number 47. Sorry Nancy...those boots were made for walking.

Top Trump – Ladybird

Weird fact you need to know: Ladybirds will be attracted to the scent of aphids, so if you've got some aphids in your garden they will act as bait for ladybird settlers. For this reason it's worth cultivating a few victim plants you don't mind being infested with aphids. They like nettles, so why not

let them settle there. At the same time, check over your more precious plants and dislodge any aphids with a spray or jet of water.

Value to the gardener: 50% Difficult to rate this one as there are other aphid predators such as the hover-fly and, of course, many other pests. However, once you've got the conditions in your garden right for ladybirds, they will be pretty much right for most other predators – apart from the larger birds, mammals and pond creatures.

Top Trump – Ladybird

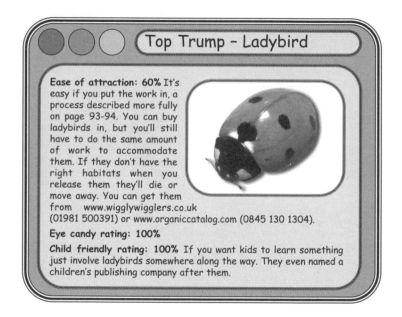

Ease of attraction: 60% It's easy if you put the work in, a process described more fully on page 93-94. You can buy ladybirds in, but you'll still have to do the same amount of work to accommodate them. If they don't have the right habitats when you release them they'll die or move away. You can get them from www.wigglywigglers.co.uk (01981 500391) or www.organiccatalog.com (0845 130 1304).

Eye candy rating: 100%

Child friendly rating: 100% If you want kids to learn something just involve ladybirds somewhere along the way. They even named a children's publishing company after them.

There are fifty species of ladybird in Britain, but one quarter of these are listed in the Red Data Book of threatened species. Loss of habitat and the use of chemical sprays is largely to blame, so again it falls to the gardener to provide a haven. Of the fifty, seven are most commonly found in gardens. You would think it would be quite easy to identify seven species. Not so...

Thanks to the ladybird's enduring popularity, most ladybird species have common names. At first glance some of them seem entirely descriptive. Names like two-spot, ten-spot and seven-spot tend to give the game away. However, of these three common garden ladybirds only the seven-spot lives up to its name. The two-spot is commonly black with two red spots, but it can also be red with no spots, or black with lots of spots. If this sounds confusing wait until you read about the ten-spot, which ranges from completely black to almost completely red with a variety of numbers of spots. The fourteen-spot doesn't have round spots. Its spots are square and quite often fused, and it's creamy-yellow and black colour sets it apart from God Almighty's Cowherd.

It is ironic that those not named after a spot count are actually easier to recognise. There is the pine ladybird (black elytra (or wing cases) with four red marks, the front pair comma shaped; the second pair more circular), the bryony (one of only two vegetarian ladybirds, it has eleven spots on an orange-red elytra) and the Australian (black elytra, orange-red apex and covered with short downy hairs). If you want to identify all fifty species, Darren J. Mann's excellent book *Ladybirds* knocks spots of this brief introduction. (OK, I promise, no more spot jokes...)

Only the ladybird knows how it manages to pick the right sub-species to mate with amidst all this visual confusion. Male ladybirds certainly mistake males for females at first introduction and will try to clamber aboard any ladybird they come across. When they realise their mistake they happily disengage and carry on with whatever they were doing before. This is all rather bumbling and opportunistic, but it seems to work. If they've guessed correctly, and if the female hasn't already mated, they will stay together for between one and eight hours. This coupling will provide just one brood per year. Ladybirds metamorphose from larvae into adults and as both larva and adult will consume several hundred aphids.

You can buy in ladybird larvae (Wiggly Wigglers and the Organic Catalogue see pages 109-110), hand pick them or tempt them in from neighbouring green spaces. However they arrive in your garden you will want them to stay and this means learning some basic rules about ladybird likes. Apart from allowing aphid reservoirs you need to start thinking about allowing a little bit of wilderness and a little bit of mess into the garden. Ladybirds love a bit of nettle, so devote an area to wild plants. This can be your sacrificial plant area for aphid colonies but will also provide the type of destination a ladybird chooses for winter retirement. If a ladybird has to leave the garden for winter it is unlikely to come back the following year.

Choose nettles, thistles, hogweed and fennel, and if you've got the space: gorse, bramble, Scots pine and ivy. You can also buy a commercial ladybird nest from the Oxford Bee Company (via CAT, see page 109). As well as your wild area you will also need to plant a good range of flowering plants around the garden that will come into bloom throughout the season. Ladybirds feed on nectar as well as pests. Just as for butterflies, buddleia is a popular choice.

All this preparation may seem like a lot of work for one predator, but the rules for ladybirds apply, with a little variation, to all insect predators, a list which includes the aphid-loving hover-fly and lacewing larvae, parasitic wasps which prey on a number of species, and, with regard to a love of wild areas, the larger predators such as hedgehogs, birds and slow-worms too.

Within each of these four 'heroes' sections you will notice a common thread of community. Just as the advice in chapter one helped sustain the soil community, the advice in this chapter will benefit the whole predator community.

Insect, arachnid and other arthropod predators, plus one gastropod

The ladybird is only one of many pest predators. Others include *Carabid* (or ground) beetles, *Straphilinid* beetles, centipedes, *Anthocorid* bugs, assassin bugs, black-kneed capsid bugs, marsh flies and hover-flies, lacewings, predatory mites, spiders and wasps. The rules for encouraging all these creatures are more or less the same as for ladybirds as described above. It is worth noting that some of them (such as ground beetles) require undisturbed ground to lay their eggs. You could devote small areas within a vegetable plot to perennial herbs.

This allows some cover for making predatory attacks and will help attract pollinators too. There are some specific strategies worth pointing out, though. Ground beetles, who dine on aphids, caterpillars and the larvae of cabbage and carrot root flies will shelter beneath small squares of felt, or similar material, placed around cabbage plants and eat the pests. Testacella slugs (identifiable by the external mussel-shaped shell on the back, near the hind end, and pinkish brown body) eat garden slugs and keel slugs and like soil with lots of organic matter. Finally, leave some small piles of rotting wood in unobtrusive corners of the garden. They provide excellent insect homes.

Parasites by post

Whereas predators eat pests or take them back to their nests to feed their young, parasites survive by making themselves at home inside, or attached to, the pest or the pest's offspring. Scientists use the rather quaint term 'host' for victims of this particularly gruesome phenomenon. The host creature will endure a variety of prolonged mutilations before eventually dying (when the guest has got what it wants and is ready to let the host perish). It's all rather gut churning but very useful for the gardener who needs a quick solution to an overwhelming pest problem.

Although all these parasitic activities happen without our assistance, it is now possible to buy in parasites and introduce them to an area with a particular pest problem. CAT supplies the slug parasite Nemaslug® but if you want to find out about the whole range of potential parasitic activity you should check out www.organiccatalog.com, or phone 0845 130 1304 for a catalogue. Here you will find parasitic controls for vine weevil, whitefly, mealy bug, leatherjacket, chafer grub and aphid. You can also buy the predators lacewing, sciarid fly and red spider mite.

Hedgehogs

If you're reading this in 2005 you'll have an extra incentive to make room for a hedgehog home in your garden – the centenary celebration of the publication of Beatrix Potter's *Tale of Mrs Tiggy-Winkle*. Not that you really need a literary milestone to pay heed to the hedgehog, it is a prolific predator of slugs, insects, baby mice and rats. Reason enough to take the necessary steps to make it feel welcome. Not to mention the fact that hedgehogs are, like so many other garden heroes, declining in number. Hedgehogs need a wild area (3m x 1.5m should be enough) with plenty of large plants and maybe a couple of brambles to feel secure, and space to make a *hibernaculum* for sleeping in through the winter months.

Traditionally, this is made from leaves tucked under a bush or log pile but you can now buy hedgehog nests, which provide the kind of stable environment they need to feel safe and confident that they will not be disturbed. TV naturalist Chris Packham suggests a home-made solution in his book *Back Garden Nature Reserve*: a metre square log camp. This is about 30-40cm high, packed with dry grass, hay and leaves and covered with a plastic tent made from some tarpaulin type material, which is further buried beneath more logs and leaves to hide the roof and provide insulation. Remember to leave room for an entrance! Hedgehogs sometimes make the mistake of making a nest in a bonfire night pile and end up a victim alongside Guy Fawkes, so always check your pyre before you start a fire. It's also worth leaving out a couple of bowls of food and water (pet food meat is ok, but never milk – it gives them diarrhoea).

Birds

This is a subject that deserves a separate book, and indeed there are many, detailing how to attract birds, what to feed them, which nests to put up to attract what bird, and so on. Birds will pretty much eat all pests from aphids up to mice and rabbits, and depending on the size of your garden you can make a home for any number of different ones. Each bird has slightly different needs but the basic requirements are: various feeding devices filled with seeds, nuts, fat and meat scraps from the kitchen; a source of water; and vantage points (usually in the form of bushes and trees) from which birds can mount attacks on their predators and to which they can escape from cats. A really good starting point is the RSPB's free brochure list, especially 'Birds in Your Garden', 'Gardening with Wildlife', 'Cats and Garden Birds' and 'Care of Sick, Injured and Orphaned Birds'. You can order them online from www.rspb.org.uk/gardens or by phoning 01767 680551. *Back Garden Nature Reserve* has some DIY bird nest plans and a series of interesting articles about the most common garden birds.

Ponds that respond

It seems that a wildlife garden makes pretty big demands on your space but actually all the suggestions in this book can be carried out in a very small area. The same can also be said of ponds. My mum has a very nice pond in half an old barrel on her concrete drive. It can't accommodate frogs but it does attract water-loving insects. If you want to cater for the full range of pond predators, including frogs, toads and bugs such as pond skaters and dragonflies, you are going to have to build something a little bigger. You can buy preformed ponds made from plastic but although it takes a little more effort you will get better results for wildlife if you form one yourself using a butyl rubber lining.

This allows you to contour the sides of the pond and make it suitable for frogs and toads to get in and out of easily. They need a gently sloping shelf about 20-30cm into the pond, which at its deepest point should be at least 60cm deep. With these dimensions you can mark out an outline with string and see if you have enough room for a fully functioning wildlife pond in your garden. Imagine how a pond will impact on the rest of your garden before you go ahead and dig one. It needs to be carefully sited so it isn't in the way of other garden activities but can still be seen from a central point in the garden. The process of building a pond is quite laborious, involving a lot of spade work mixed with moments demanding great patience and an ability to get measurements and calculations right. If you're up for the job look for a book on ponds or DIY projects in the garden, or a good wildlife book like Chris Packham's. If not, contact a wildlife garden designer or gardener who specialises in wildlife ponds. If you go to the expense of hiring a contractor you want to know that they will do the job properly. If you aren't sure about the sincerity of their appreciation of wildlife ask to see evidence of similar work. A good designer and gardener should have a portfolio of work with photographs.

Part Two
The Directory

Mail order companies

A whole range of products are now available to help you garden for wildlife. Here are just some of the companies who supply them.

- Centre for Alternative Technology Mail Order, Machynlleth, Powys, SY20 9AZ; 01654 705959; www.cat.org.uk
  Wide range of books and products including *The Little Book of Slugs*, Nemaslug® and Oxford Bee Company Bee, Butterfly and Ladybug boxes.
- Natural History Book Service, 2-3 Wills Road, Totnes, Devon TQ9 5XN, 01803 865913, www.nhbs.com
  Wide range of books about wildlife for those interested in finding out more.
- The Organic Catalogue, Chase Organics, River Dene Business Park, Molesey Road, Hersham, Surrey, KT12 4RG; 0845 130 1304; www.organiccatalog.com
  Wide range of organic pest control products, organic seeds,

comfrey root cuttings, books and associated garden materials and equipment.
- Wiggly Wigglers, Lower Blakemere Farm, Blakemere, Herefordshire, HR2 9PX; 01981 500391; www.wigglywigglers.co.uk
  Wide range of compost products, including wormeries and worms, bird houses and food (live worms, seeds and specially prepared fat balls and fruit and nut feed bars) and bug boxes.

Membership Organisations

All these groups help to protect and popularise garden heroes. Most of them provide advice services, helplines, books and products. Many carry out yearly surveys to monitor populations of species and will help you identify your garden heroes.

- Bat Conservation Trust, 15 Cloisters House, 8 Battersea Park Road, London, SW8 4BG; 020 7627 2629; www.bats.org.uk

- Bees, Wasps and Ants Recording Society, Nightingales, Halsmere Road, Surrey, GU8 5BN; www.bwars.com
- British Arachnological Society, Membership Treasurer, 71 Havant Road, Walthamstow, London, E17 3JE; www.britishspiders.org.uk; membership@britishspiders.org.uk
- British Dragonfly Society, Membership Office, Barbados House, Station Road, Borden, Hants, GU35 0LR; www.dragonflysoc.org.uk; belinda@broadwaypark.freeserve.co.uk
- British Entomological and Natural History Society, c/o The Pelham-Clinton Building, Dinton Pastures Country Park, Davis Street, Hurst, Reading, Berkshire, RG10 0TH; www.benhs.org.uk
- British Hedgehog Preservation Society, Hedgehog House, Dhustone, Ludlow, Shropshire, SY8 3PL; 01584 890801; www.software-technics.com/bhps; bhps@dhustone.fsbusiness. co.uk;
- Botanical Society of the British Isles, 41 Marlborough Road, Roath, Cardiff, CF23 5BU; www.bsbi.org.uk

- Buglife – The Invertebrate Conservation Trust, 170A Park Road, Peterborough, Cambridgeshire, PE21 2UF; 01733 201210; www.buglife.org.uk; matt.shardlow@buglife.org.uk
- Butterfly Conservation, Manor Yard, East Lulworth, Wareham, Dorset BH20 5QP; 01929 400209; www.butterfly-conservation.org; info@butterfly-conservation.org
- Froglife, White Lodge, London Road, Peterborough, PE7 0LG; 01733 558844; www.froglife.org; info@froglife.org
- HDRA – The Organic Organisation, Ryton Gardens, Coventry, Warwickshire, CV8 3LG; 024 7630 3517; www.hdra.org.uk; enquiry@hdra.org.uk
- Hedgehog Helpline, 5 Foreland Road, Whitchurch, Cardiff, CF14 7AR; 029 2062 3985; www.hedgehg-dircon.co.uk/hedgehogs; hedgehog@dircom.co.uk
- The Herb Society, Sulgrave Manor, Sulgrave, Banbury, OX17 2SD; 01295 768899; www.herbsociety.co.uk; email@herbsociety.co.uk
- International Bee Research Association, 18 North Road, Cardiff, CF10 3DT; 029 2037 2409; www.ibra.org.uk; mail@ibra.org.uk

- The National Beekeeping Centre, NAC, Stoneleigh Park, Warwickshire, CV8 2LG; 02476 696679; www.bbka.org.uk; bbka@britishbeekeepers.com
- Plantlife, 14 Rollestone Street, Salisbury, Wiltshire, SP1 1DX; 01722 342730 www.plantlife.org.uk; enquiries@plantlife.org.uk
- Ponds Conservation Trust, BMS, Oxford Brookes University, Gipsy Lane, Headington, Oxford, OX3 0BP; 01865 483 249; www.pondstrust.org.uk; info@pondstrust.org.uk
- Royal Society for the Protection of Birds, The Lodge, Sandy, Bedfordshire, SG19 2DL; 01767 680551; www.rspb.org.uk
- St Tiggywinkles, Aston Road, Haddenham, Aylesbury, Buckinghamshire, HP17 8AF; 01844 292292; www.sttiggywinkles.org.uk; mail@sttiggywinkles.org.uk
- The Tree Council, 71 Newcomen Street, London, SE1 1YT; 020 7407 9992; www.treecouncil.org.uk; info@treecouncil.org.uk
- Wildflower Society, 82a High Street, Sawston, Cambridge, CB2 4HJ; 01223 830665; http://rbg-web2.rbge.org.uk/wfsoc; wfs@grantais.demon.co.uk

- The Wildlife Trusts, The Kiln, Waterside, Mather Road, Newark, Nottinghamshire, NG24 1WT; 0870 0367711; www.wildlifetrusts.org
- World Wide Fund for Nature, Panda House, Weyside Park, Godalming, Surrey, GU7 1XR; 01483 426444; www.wwf.org.uk

For more, visit the excellent Natural History Museum website www.nhm.ac.uk/naturenavigator and www.animalrescuers.co.uk

Bibliography and Further Reading

Books

- *A Green History of The World*, Clive Ponting, Sinclair Stevenson (available to order from the US via www.amazon.co.uk at various prices)
- *Bumble-bees*, Christopher O'Toole, Osmia Publications, £4.95
- *Back Garden Nature Reserve*, Chris Packham, The Wildlife Trusts/New Holland Publishers, £14.99

- *Bob Flowerdew's Organic Bible*, Bob Flowerdew, Kyle Cathie Ltd, £14.99
- *Comfrey: Past, Present and Future*, Lawrence D. Hills, Faber Paperbacks (not in print but second hand copies available through www.amazon.co.uk)
- *Creative Sustainable Gardening*, Diana Anthony, CAT, £12.99
- *High Tide – News From a Warming World*, Mark Lynas, Flamingo, £16.99
- *How to Make Soil and Save Earth*, Allan Shepherd, CAT, £4.99
- *Ladybirds*, Darren Mann, Osmia Publications, £4.95
- *Minibeasts in the Garden*, English Nature, (free)
- *No-nonsense Guide to Climate Change*, Dinyar Godrej, New Internationalist, £7.00
- *Start with the Soil*, Grace Gershuny, Rodale Press, £7.99
- *The Complete Manual of Organic Gardening*, Basil Caplan, Headline (out of print)
- *The Little Book of Slugs*, Allan Shepherd and Suzanne Galant, CAT, £4.99
- *The Natural Garden Book*, Gia (out of print)

- *The Natural History of the Garden*, Michael Chinery, Collins (out of print)
- *The Red Mason Bee*, Christopher O'Toole, Osmia Publications, £4.95
- *The RHS Encyclopedia of Herbs and Their Uses*, Deni Bown, Dorling Kindersley, £30.00
- *The Soil*, Davies, Walker *et al*, Harper Collins (out of print)
- *The Song of the Dodo*, David Quammen, Hutchinson (available in paperback from Pimlico) £17.00

All books listed here and not out of print are available from CAT on 01654 705959 or www.cat.org.uk (ask for postage rates).

Websites

Introduction
www.amnh.org
www.dodopad.com
www.bbc.co.uk
www.rhs.org.uk

Composters
www.soils.usda.gov
www.ladybird-survey.pwp.blueyonder.co.uk
www.digitalseed.com/composter
www.interactive.usask.ca
www.ohioline.osu.edu
www.earthlife.net/insects
www.enchantedlearning.com

www.webmesh.co.uk/darwinworms.htm/1
www.rain.org
www.ag.usask.ca
www.encyclopedia.com/html/w1/worm.asp
www.wildaboutgardens.org

Pollinators
www.butterfly-conservation.org
www.mystical-www.co.uk
www.sccf.org
www.lincstrust.co.uk
www.butterflyplants.co.uk
www.chebucto.ns.ca/~ag151/bee_tidbits.html

Plants
www.futurefoods.com
www.purplesage.org.uk
www.greenchronicle.com
www.hdra.org.uk

www.organicnutrition.co.uk
www.pfaf.org
www.botanical.com
www.planetherbs.com
www.wicken.org.uk
www.healthreaction.com

Predators
www.uksafari.com
www.earthlife.net
www.herballegacy.com
www.rspb.org.uk
www.wildlifetrusts.org
www.garden-birds.co.uk
www.software-technics.co.uk/bhps
www.hedghogz.co.uk
www.guardian.co.uk
www.wildlondon.org.uk
www.overthegardengate.net
www.thehedgehog.co.uk

Appendix

Garden Chemicals

At the end of 2003, a number of pesticides were withdrawn from sale as a result of an EC review programme that was designed to make sure that all pesticides on sale are safe. The last day on which they could be sold was 24 July 2003.

The reason for the withdrawal of the products was that they were not supported commercially, and because safety concerns have been identified. Commercial withdrawal of pesticide products is common (none of these currently withdrawn chemicals have been taken off the market for safety reasons).

The last day for storage of these chemicals (for the purposes of disposal only) was 31 March 2004.

If you inadvertently keep or use any withdrawn chemicals any prosecution action against you is a matter for your local authority. The maximum fine for pesticide offences is £5000.

Products that you have in your garden shed, such as:

- Moss and weed killers for lawns and paths
- Treatments for removing algae from decking and patios
- Ant, cockroach, fly, wasp and aphid killers
- Slug pellets
- Mice and rat poisons
- Anti-mould and fungus paints
- Timber treatments

could contain banned chemicals, such as:

- Dichlorprop
- Dikegulac
- Resmethrin
- 2,3,6-TBA
- Tar acids
- Triforine

If your garden shed contains anything labelled as having one or more of the six substances mentioned above, make sure to dispose of them safely. It's illegal to dispose of garden chemicals or their wastes to drains, sinks or lavatories. Your local waste disposal authority, i.e. your County Council or Unitary Council, will be able to advise you on where and how to dispose of them.

For more information, see:
www.pesticides.gov.uk
www.pan-uk.org
www.environment-agency.gov.uk